Was I in Mama's Stomach, Too?

Dagmar Geisler

Translated by
Andrea Jones Berasaluce

Sky Pony Press
New York

Published by arrangement with Loewe Verlag GmbH.
Title of the original German edition: *War ich auch in
Mamas Bauch?*
© 2014 Loewe Verlag GmbH, Bindlach

10 9 8 7 6 5 4 3 2 1

Manufactured in China, June 2019
This product conforms to CPSIA 2008

Library of Congress Cataloging-in-Publication Data
is available on file.

Cover provided by Loewe Verlag GmbH
Cover illustration by Dagmar Geisler

Print ISBN: 978-1-5107-4652-7
Ebook ISBN: 978-1-5107-4663-3

Lili, one of Mama's coworkers, visited us today. Lili has a very round, rather large belly.

"There's a baby growing in there. It'll be born soon," Mama explained.

"Will it be a boy or a girl?"

"I don't know yet," Lili told me.

After Lili left, I asked Mama, "Was I in your stomach, too?"

"Of course!" Mama said.

"And was your stomach as round as Lili's?"

Mama laughed. "I think my stomach was even rounder. You were a big baby when you came into the world. Twenty-one and a half inches long and nearly nine pounds."

You had this
on after
your birth.

On the bracelet
it states your
name and
birthdate.

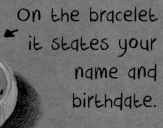

"Was your stomach that thick the whole time?" I asked.

"No, no!" Mama said. "In the beginning, it wasn't visible at all. You were as small as a pea at first. Here, look: the small dot on the ultrasound image is the first I saw of you. Because of this, I knew for sure that I was pregnant."

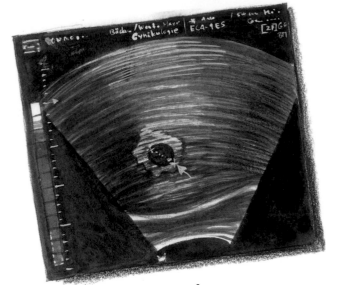

The first ↑
ultrasound
image of you.

Here is the ultrasound on the computer screen. That was exciting!

"Who took the picture?" I asked.

"My doctor did. She also gave me a little booklet. It's called a maternity log. Every time she examined me, she wrote down what had changed between appointments."

Grandma sewed this pretty cover for my maternity log.

"In the beginning there was only an egg cell," Mama explained. "It was no larger than a period in a book. It divided and divided until it became a clump of cells.

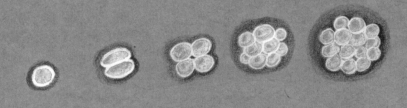

The small clump wandered into the stomach through the fallopian tubes in the uterus. There it settled to keep growing. All this happened before I even knew I was having a baby."

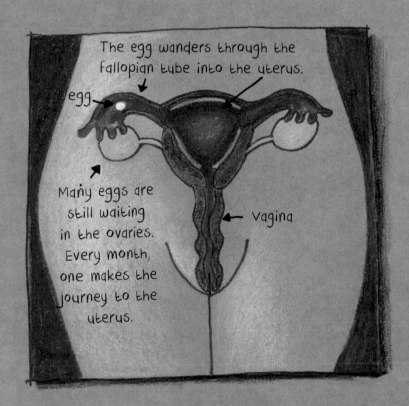

The egg wanders through the fallopian tube into the uterus.

egg

Many eggs are still waiting in the ovaries. Every month, one makes the journey to the uterus.

Vagina

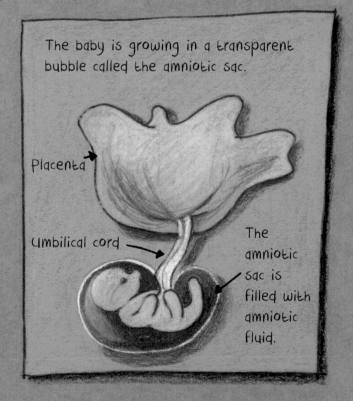

The baby is growing in a transparent bubble called the amniotic sac.

Placenta

Umbilical cord

The amniotic sac is filled with amniotic fluid.

"When I found out I was pregnant with you, you were the size of that chocolate candy. You looked like a little worm."

"Even after five weeks, you were only as big as a pinhead. We could only have seen you using a microscope.

After eight weeks, you were as big as a gummy bear. Your heart was beating, but you didn't look like a baby yet.

By three months, you were about the size of this hard candy."

"In the fourth month, you were about as big as the doll from your dollhouse. Hair slowly grew on your head, and you could blink and suck your thumb.

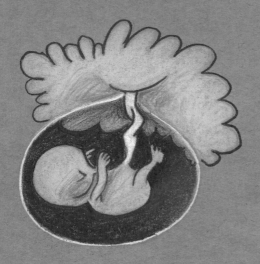

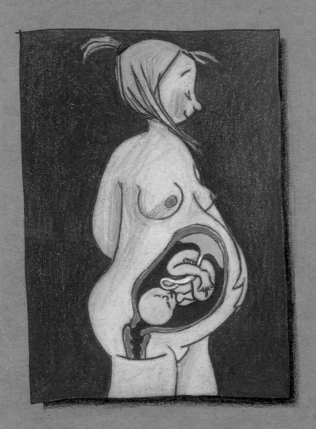

In the fifth month, you were as long as a brand-new colored pencil. You already looked like a real baby! But you still had a bit more growing to do.

It takes about nine months for a baby to finish growing. Shortly before birth, you were heavier than thirty bars of chocolate."

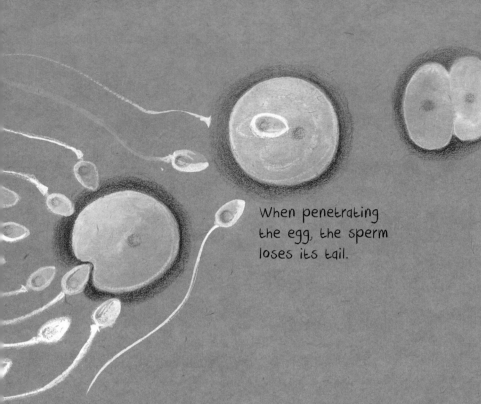

The nucleus of the sperm cell and the egg merge together, and then the egg is able to divide and divide and divide . . .

When penetrating the egg, the sperm loses its tail.

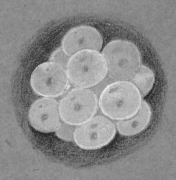

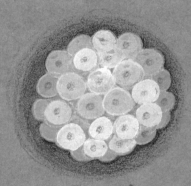

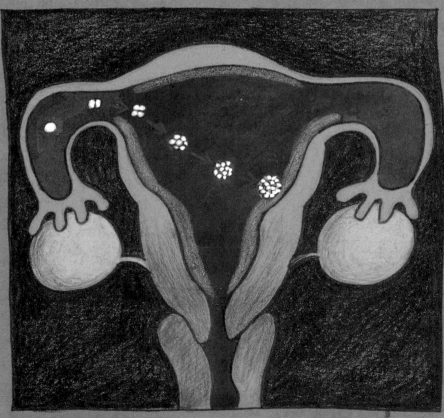

The fertilized egg migrates to the uterus. There, it nestles in to continue growing.

"When the semen reaches the egg cell, the cell starts to divide, again and again, until it has formed a small cell clump, which continues to migrate until it nestles into the uterus."

"I already know that!" I said.

"The man's sperm swims in a white fluid called semen," Dad continues. "In the semen are thousands of sperm cells. They all make their way simultaneously through the vagina into the uterus and then into the fallopian tube. Each one wants to reach the egg that is making its way from the ovary to the uterus. This happens only once a month, and so it's mostly luck when a sperm finds an egg it can fertilize."

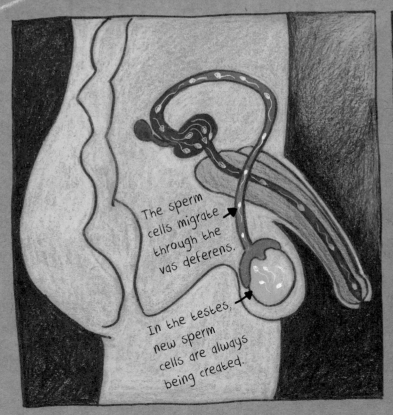

The sperm cells migrate through the vas deferens.

In the testes, new sperm cells are always being created.

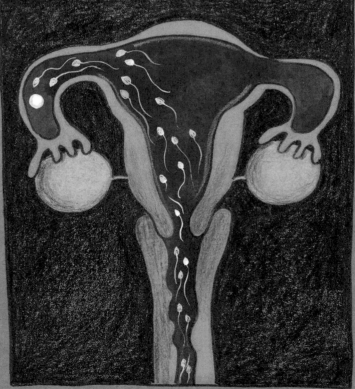

The sperm cells make their way through the vagina and the uterus to the fallopian tubes. They are racing; only the first sperm—the quickest—is allowed to fertilize the egg.

"When both consent, adults like to touch each other in the places where they are different," explained Dad. "The man likes to caress the woman's breasts and vagina. The woman strokes the man's penis. The penis becomes big and very stiff.

Then, the man pushes his penis into the woman's vagina. And he keeps moving it in and out. It's a nice feeling. The most beautiful part happens when the man's semen flows into the woman's vagina.

Afterward, the two are mostly tired, and they snuggle together and fall asleep."

"Boring!" I said.

"I don't think so," Dad said. He smiled and gave Mama a kiss.

"And now how does the baby get in the stomach?" I asked.

"Adults in love, they want to . . .

. . . and caress . . .

. . . kiss constantly . . .

. . . and cuddle."

"Well," Dad began, "traditionally, you need a man and a woman who are in love. It also works without being in love. But it's much nicer when in love."

Dad continued: "Men and women are different in a few places. Women have breasts, labia, and a vagina. Men have a penis and a scrotum."

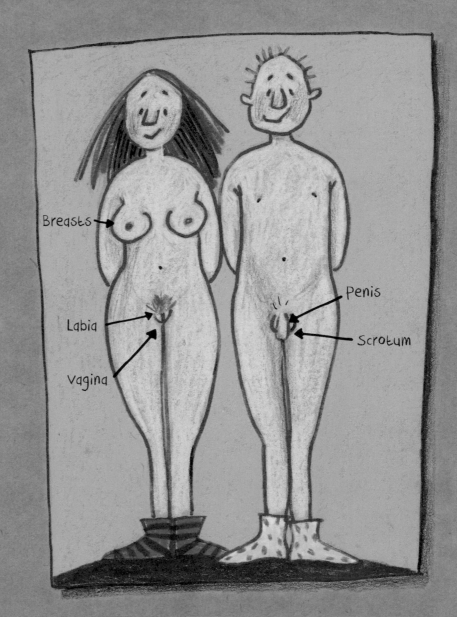

"Hm," I said. "Now I know that I was in your stomach and I know how I got out of it. But how did I get in there in the first place?"

At that moment, we heard a sound at the door. Dad was home!

"Hello!" Mama called cheerfully. "Our child wants to know how babies come to be in the stomach."

"Aha," Dad said. "Well, I can explain that."

"Me too!" said Mama.

"But now it's Dad's turn!" I said. "You already explained everything else."

"And then we were both exhausted and fell asleep."

"Daddy too?" I asked.

"I don't think so. He was still too excited from this thrilling adventure!" Mama said.

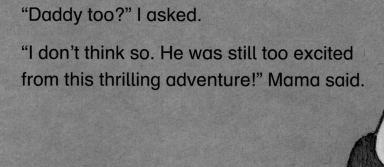

"Dad was allowed to cut the umbilical cord."

"Did that hurt?" I ask.

"No, not at all," said Mama.

"You were hungry shortly after birth, so I fed you milk from my breast for the first time."

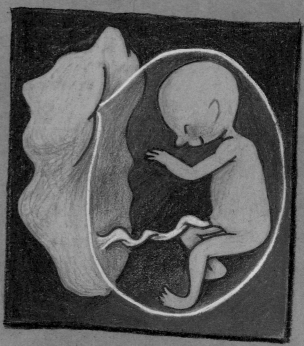

In the stomach, the baby gets its food via the umbilical cord. Through the blood, it gets some of everything the mother eats.

"At some point, the contractions became more frequent, and the amniotic sac that you'd been living in burst. Then you came out, headfirst through the vagina. The vagina actually stretches enough for a baby to pass through during birth."

"The uterus contracts,
over and over again.
It hurts; that's why they're
called labor pains," Mama said.
"First there's a contraction, and then
there's a pause so you can recover. When
Dad and I arrived at the birth house, I had already had many contractions. That's why we thought
you'd arrive soon. But it took a few hours.

Luckily, the nice midwife at the birth house was on duty, and she had already taught us everything about the birth process. 'It'll be fine!' she said.

Dad and I walked up and down the hallway for a while and I rocked on the exercise ball a bit."

"When labor started, it was the middle of the night. We hurried to get to the birth house in time. Dad grabbed two different socks out of excitement and put his sweater on wrong."

"How did you notice that it had started?" I asked Mama.

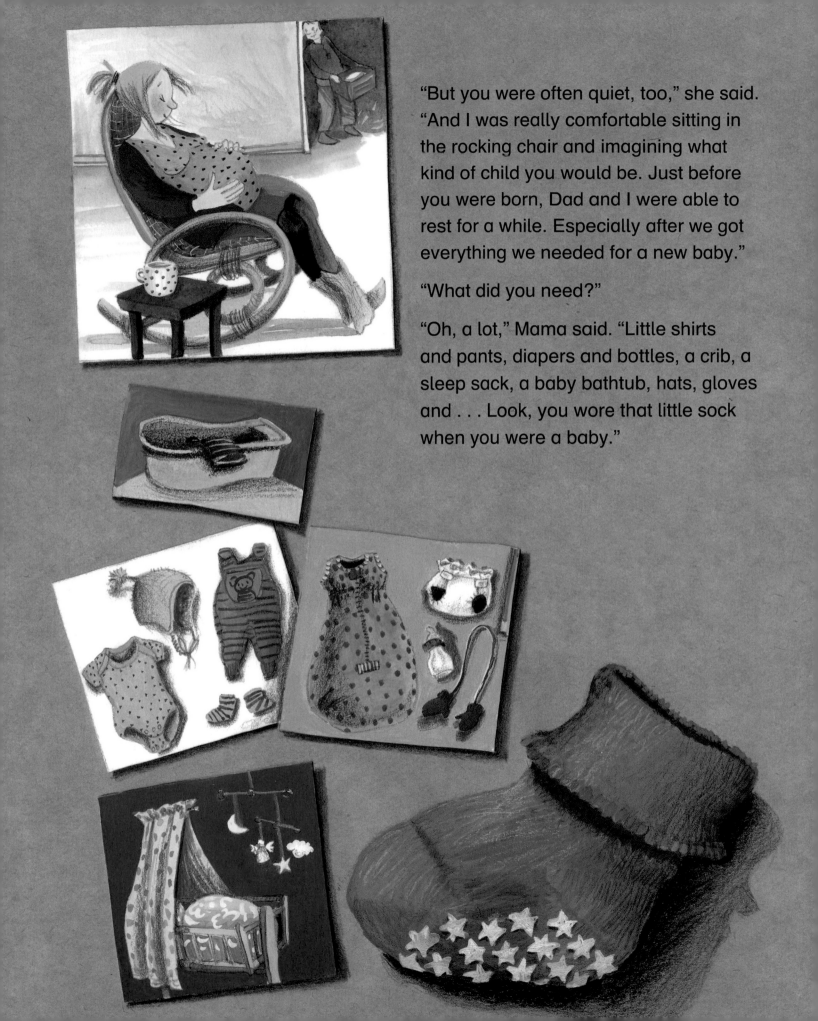

"But you were often quiet, too," she said. "And I was really comfortable sitting in the rocking chair and imagining what kind of child you would be. Just before you were born, Dad and I were able to rest for a while. Especially after we got everything we needed for a new baby."

"What did you need?"

"Oh, a lot," Mama said. "Little shirts and pants, diapers and bottles, a crib, a sleep sack, a baby bathtub, hats, gloves and . . . Look, you wore that little sock when you were a baby."

"Over time, my belly kept growing. Just before your birth, I was so big that it was hard for me to go up the stairs or tie my shoes. And at night, you sometimes punched and kicked so gleefully that I couldn't sleep."

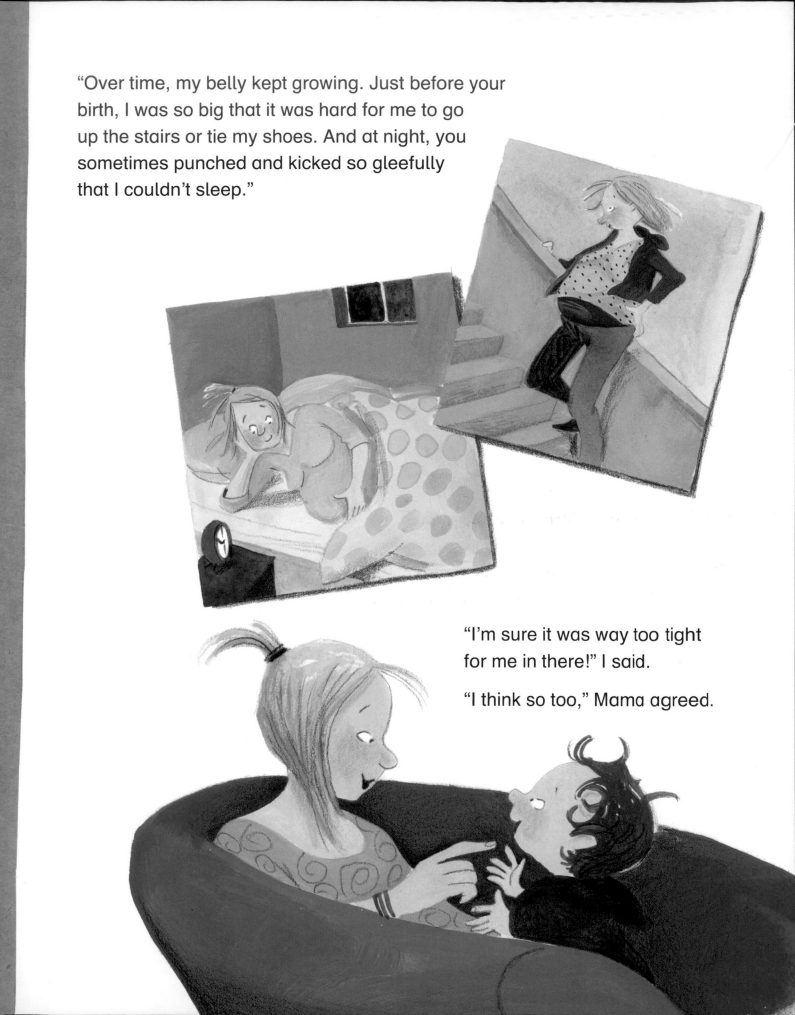

"I'm sure it was way too tight for me in there!" I said.

"I think so too," Mama agreed.